Love-Sonnets,

by

Evelyn Douglas.

Τὸ μέλημα τοὐμόν

Sappho, frag 126

Beauty.

BEAUTY is liberal as the heavenly air,
   Beauty is boundless as the universe :
  The waves of evil ponderously immerse
The pearl of good ; beauty is everywhere.
Beauty is a devout a deep despair ;
   Hopes that with heaven's highest stars converse :
   The poisonous blossom of a devil's curse,
The first and last word of an angel's prayer
Creation and destruction at thy beck
   Call love and lust · through battle's bloody swarm
   That youth with smiling face sees but thy form
And, 'mid the shrieks of the fast sinking wreck,
A poet, standing on the wave-washed deck,
   Stares awe-struck at the beauty of the storm.

Aug 7th, 1888

I.

L^O iu thine honour I will build a place
    Wheie thou and I may dwell with love apart,
  Hand clasped in hand and beating heart to heart,
And find from life's dull tumult a sweet space
Of rest and quiet : on its walls I trace
  Shapes of religious and devoted art
  And hues of fair imaginings, that start
And fill each crevice with thy sudden face.
Come live in it, for it is thine ; thy friend
  Is but the architect. 'Tis dark : so come,
    Reveal its form with thine indwelling smile.
Nor lack I some far hope that in the end
  Thy memory may thine heritor become,
    And live in this pure house a little while.

II.

SINCE I have known you I have little heed
    For care or pain or fear.   While we two live
  Present or absent, we can richly give
Peace to each other.   Hearts will run to weed
Like ruined gardens, scanted of love's seed.
  Not ours · there sun and rain, restorative,
    Awake the flowers , there heavenly smiles forgive
The errors of the rankest growth they breed.
Ah love me ever · pardon every wrong
    That makes thy garden look less beautiful,
      Even our love my soul should free of tares—
A slothful husbandman, whose idle song
    Alas too often leaves the rich soil dull,
      Stealing its dues of toil : but love forbears

III.

THE primal earth, the all-pervading skies,
    The moon that at the sun her wan lip warms,
  The stars and all we guess of them, the swarms
Of meteors, mists that melt in rainbow dyes,
The ocean and its world of far-off sighs,
    The forest and its voices, the vague forms
    Of mountains in green twilight, wingéd storms
That like red eagles from the sunset rise,
The living things that through their love and hate
  Interpret these by vision to their thought,
    And man that speaks his thought in words, I see;
And these with life, and death, and love, and fate,
  And all conceptions of my soul, in-wrought,
    Make up the complex whole, my dream of thee

IV.

WHY do I love the silence of the moon,
    The paradisal distance of the dawn,
   The depth of eve mysteriously withdrawn,
Better than all the roses of late June,
The garden's breath, the orchard's golden boon,
    The burning brightness of the new-mown lawn,
    The mossy forest-floor with beech-mast strawn,
And green trees waving in the depth of noon.
Night hath her dreams and the lone heart its tears;
    Silence and longing weep themselves to rest
    Each on the other's mild and maiden breast;
The seeking spirit sighs, the dim star hears;
    Distance and high devotion suit the best,
And deep as thy deep eyes the dawn appears.

V.

JOY in desire more than desire of jóy
    Hath ever been my passion : mute from far
  To love an unknown woman like a star ;
To build in dreams no waking could destroy
Some island-palace far from life's annoy ;
  By strength of spirit to force the silver bar
  Of twilight till the dawn-gates stood ajar,
And gaze on Paradise, a dazzled boy ;
To look forth o'er the ocean's grey-lit foam
  In the dim morning, and in starry night
    Upon the myriad-mustered worlds above ;
To emulate the unequalled, Greece and Rome,
  Heroes and deeds, the heads of faith and fight ;
    To adore thee whom I may scarcely love.

VI.

HOW oft a lover in his later age
  Turning the leaves of some young poet's book
 With idle finger and far absent look,
Startled, hath seen glance up from the clear page
A thought once deemed his sole self-heritage,
  But left forgotten in some leafy nook,
  When youth and love, locked hand in hand, forsook
His faltering steps on life's long pilgrimage.
Ah tears break forth that ever this should be—
  Love like a glorious vision rearise,
As if the sunset rose above the sea.
  And I, how leapt my heart with mad surprise,
  When, stooping down to kiss thee, from thine eyes
I saw my own lost soul look up at me.

VII.

THE perfume hidden at the rose's heart ;
　　The inner sweetness of a dream ; the cry
　Of sorrow that escapes within a sigh,
The love within a kiss ; the soul's keen smart
Hid in a tear ; the spiritual counterpart
　Of a swift meaning motion of the eye,
　Or lights that on the lips are born and die,
Named smiles :—all this to me and more thou art.
Search in thy breast, and see what holiest thing
　Dwells inmost of thy thoughts, fulfilling each,
　A soul unto the body of thy speech :
Then I in thee, as thou in me, shall sing,
　　And heaven in both, and both in heaven's reach—
Skies in our heart and skies about our wing.

VIII

HAST thou, lone-standing by the forest's verge,
    Marked the mysterious melody that sweeps
   Among the boughs, or, melancholy, creeps
Along the moss ? or felt the dismal dirge,—
High up on mountain summits, that emerge
    Above the reign of storm, where the snow sleeps,—
   Of the unquiet distant ocean-deeps
At the sky's edge of shining stars and surge ?
So dim a music from so deep a source
    Hath my love's voice to me, as if it spake
     Out of the earth or from beyond the spheres .
Lost hope, and vain regret, and long remorse
    Out of the heart's deep solitudes awake   [tears.
     Like the world's dead, and clothe themselves with

IX.

HOW love ran on with us his varying course
　　From distant worship on to close embrace,
　　Would be a tale might drench the sternest face
With pitying tears : how sweet the joy could force
Our reticence ; how came the long divorce
　　That left our hearts alone a weary space
　　Moaning apart each in his prison-place ;
How bitter at the end our vain remorse ;
What heart-aches and what tears, what long reproach,
　　What disappointments, sleep-forsaken nights,
　　　And mornings when to wake was a regret ;
What long disgust to watch the sun encroach
　　Upon the zenith, creeping up the heights,
　　　What loathing hate of life to see him set.

A leaf upon the river : let it float
　　With the loitering tide by many a winding reach
　Under the grassy banks, past many a beach
Of silvery silt and shingle !　The waves lift
Lazily on through lights that cross and shift
　　And dancing shadows, where the birch and beech
　　High up their leaning loving boughs impleach,
Then sweep it down the mill-race sudden and swift.
A heart that dallies with love's luring tide
　　Dancing with soft pulsation, lightly afloat
　　　Upon the rising and subsiding wave,
Borne on through sun and shadow . let it glide,
　　Till helpless as a hurricane-harried boat
　　　It hear the deafening waters rush and rave.

XI.

WHY are we thus divided having kissed ?
    Why are we yet two bodies and not one ?
  Why have our separate spirits leave to run
Two sundered paths of thought ? what laws resist
The perfect bond whereof we dimly wist ?
    Love, incomplete, seems ever but begun,
    And yearns to consummation never won,
His purpose always nearly gained,—and missed.
As mournful waves with desolate delight
That moaning kiss the same sands night by night
    In changeless hunger, and are not appeased :
So I, who famish at possession's goal,
Must kiss and kiss, yet kisses ne'er console
    Love's over-burdened heart that is not eased.

XII.

L^O every leaf that dances in the glades
  Hath some soft shadow, that, swift and close as speech
 Attends on thought, reflects it (Mark how each
Of those transparent delicate purple shades
Flutters and trembles, deepens and then fades
 Along the silver bark of the smooth beech,
 As waxing or as waning light may teach)—
Two beating hearts one sympathy pervades.
Thought is twin-born, the magnet's double pole ;
 And as one leaning o'er a well descries
  Reflections mount of things he cannot see,
So I, down-gazing in my own stilled soul
 At quietest, have beheld t'ward me arise
  As shapes in water, the thoughts that pass in thee.

XIII.

TO see the shadow and the leaf commune
    And pulse for pulse tremulously reply,—
  Like dancing butterfly to butterfly,
As if two beating hearts beat to one tune,—
I wish that our two spirits therein were mewn,
    Thou in the leaf, in the fond shadow I,
    In sunny summer woods when winds were high,
One double heart-beat in the breast of June.
Nay thou shouldst be a cloud to float and rest
    In bluest ether mid transcendent light,
    And I a shadow to pursue thy flight
O'er flower-spread plain and green hill's rounded breast;
    Or thou shouldst be a sweet song in the night,
And I an answering echo scarcely guessed.

XIV

KISSES are sweetest under covering hair,
  And whispers in its woven twilight best;
 As flowery boughs above the chirping nest
Make sweet and sacred all the darkened air
Wherein abide the soft-secluded pair,
  And know in the warm fragrance where they rest
  The small heart beating in the downy breast
Each of its mate :—a Paradise they share.
This is a longing of the human heart
  After that dream, an Eden all for two,
  Some lonely island 'mid the ocean's blue
Where Love may sport, and laugh, and kiss apart.
  Therefore it was a moment past I drew
Thine hair about mine eyes, Eve that thou art

XV.

TWO bubbles in a crystal bowl appear,
  Born separately : round the opposing rims
  Each for awhile in a charmed circle swims,
And shuns the other's touch, as if in fear.
A gold-fish rising breaks the mimic mere ,
  A thwart tide, traversing the surface, dims
  The placid water · from the distant brims
The bubbles swept together are one sphere !
They might have perished singly ; might have known
  Life but not love, and living separate
  Have ceased imperfect, sundered mate from mate ;
And thou and I have walked the world alone,
And died so, if the strong storm had not blown
  That swept us hither on the tides of Fate.

XVI.

THE slumberous stillness of the summer noon,
   Is not its drowsy quiet perfect peace ?
  The very voices of the children cease
From their sweet laughter, as in dreamful swoon
They sink back in the grass, outwearied soon
   With play and pleasure through the light's increase.
  Night hath no hour like this in all her lease
Of cold calm slumber 'neath the spell-bound moon.
So is the height of love a perfect rest,
   And stiller than all frost that ever froze
  The ice-bound river, or sleep of spotless snows
On inaccessible mountain's footless crest,
   Lies the all-peaceful glow, the warm repose,
Of loving heart on heart, and breast by breast.

XVII.

THE poor dumb creatures of the field, that call
    So sadly to their young ; whose narrow mind,
    Consciously helpless, looks up to mankind
Through pleading piteous eyes ; that live in thrall,
Or, stricken in the shambles, groaning fall :—
    Thinking of these how little grace they find,
    And then of thee who never wast unkind,
And of our love, I could weep for them all.
This is the gift of Love, that we, so blest,
    Should feel for the afflicted ; that we twain
    Should be united against wrong and pain,
The slaughtered lamb, the wild bird's rifled nest,
    And, most of all, the fraud and force that stain
Homes of the human poor and the oppressed.

XVIII.

THE rifled riches of some flowery mead
    Strewn by the roadside, scorned and castaway ;
  A bird's nest, pilfered on a holiday,
Its blue eggs broken, left with little heed ;—
Such things have ever made my heart to bleed,
  Nay, I have oft stood still in mute dismay,
  As o'er a young life's ruins, prone to say
Had he a mother once who did this deed ?
Ah cruel longing changed for crueller scorn :
  Ah tears despised and modesty defaced
  By ruthless wanton cruelty and waste :
From matron shame the virgin sweetness torn
  To die at leisure having loved in haste ;
And beauty blighted ere it could be born.

XIX.

SWEET lady mine, behold this desolate world ·
    The little children go with weeping face,
    And women, that sowed love to reap disgrace,
Walk the cold streets with lips grown cruel and curled :
Falsehood like lime into the dark air hurled
    Blinds the dim eyes of men : in frantic race
    For wealth, the noble are trampled by the base :
The red street runs, the red flag flies unfurled.
Sweet lady, kisses for a little while,
    And then who knows what end for thee and me
      Who cannot bear these things, nor walk these ways ?
Ah make me brave enough with thy dear smile
    For the truth's sake to leave both it and thee.
    But woe for Love born in these latter days.

XX.

" NOBLESSE oblige :" it was a simple creed,
    Forgotten now, that who preferred a claim
  To life more honoured than the general name
Should give it for the general good at need .
And from this outworn faith arose a breed
    Of men who sickened at the thought of shame,
    Whose swords, kept bright by use, were fire to tame
On England's soil the growth of waste and weed.
He who has once loved truly is a knight,
    Knows deep down in his heart heroic worth,
      And pins upon his crest a lady's glove.
Him shall you not turn back in the grim fight
    Uncover and own then, ye who prate of birth,
      The untitled aristocracy of Love.

XXI.

LOVE is own brother to self-sacrifice ;
    And in his happiest hour there is a breath
   That sweeps him on tumultuously to death.
The heart that has not loved is cold as ice ,
Lovers will sooner leave their paradise
    Than such an one his joyless gloom, that saith
    Wait for the bright day though it tarrieth.
Love freely gives up Love, a priceless price.
In Love's heart burns a self-destroying fire,
    A heavenward, suicidal, soaring flame .
From the doomed barque Love looks forth with desire
On the grand surf-line drawing ever nigher :
    The loveless hug their loneliness and shame ;
Love lights the marriage-bed, a glorious pyre.

XXII.

LOVE is a path to virtue for the brave
   Led by the beautiful; a great desire
  In souls that are not perfect, but aspire
After perfection; a high hope to save
The noble heart from world-stains that deprave
  Its purity, to lift it from the mire
  And cleanse it through with agony and fire
Fit for a new life entered through the grave.
For even where no hero sheds his blood
The young tree suffers to produce the bud,
  The parent through the offspring withereth:
And where no sweet soul bleeds to death in song
The body's pangs the bodily life prolong,
  And birth is to the mother a sweet death.

XXIII.

LOVED once for ever loved : how surely sounds
    This gospel to me since I learned to list
Truth from thy lips, mine own evangelist.
What thought presumes to set now any bounds
To Love whose being informs us and surrounds ?
    Yes, I am now become Love's pantheist;
    In him and by him men, his shows, subsist,
And to his glory all we do redounds.
Our life's one purpose is to see his might
    Shine through appearance, and to live by it :
His bonds are free, his duty a delight ;
Linked with his law our lives shall move aright,
    Harmoniously with all creation knit ,
And death itself shall dawn to fuller light.

XXIV.

THE sea's wide bounds are yet not wide enough.
　　Have you not heard it fret, as if, coerced
　In so small space, its mighty heart would burst ?
And shall one human breast find room for love ?
Love that lights all the firmament above,
　　The want wherewith the suns and systems thirst,
　　The end and the beginning, last and first
Of all things, God embodied in a Dove.
Ay, in one point meet two infinitudes,
　　And Love can live as readily in my heart,
　　Though narrower than a needle's viewless dart,
As, through the uncircumscribed star-multitudes
　　Pervading utmost heaven in every part,
Make habitable its populous solitudes.

XXV.

LOVE'S folly in others seemeth such no less
    To foolish lovers, as if one should sneer,
   Passing, to see his mirrored face appear,
And in such things to blame is to confess.
But when love's passionate wrongs cry for redress
   Or true love's tragic wisdom earns a tear,
   Young noble hearts in happier fate draw near
And prove by grief their right to happiness.
O Love, in thee, as in one faith, unite
    The chiefly blest with the supremely cursed,
     And pity proves their high community ;
     One brotherhood of human deity.
    Who knows then but the last may yet be first,
So thou but lead me, Love, with thy dear light ?

XXVI.

THERE is a secret all true lovers share,
   A mystery none initiate ever names,
  And none shall ever know whom love disclaims,
Whereby his votaries breathe a common air,
And know each other and themselves. Forbear,
   Ye alien lives whom honest passion shames,
   And ye whose bodily lust obscures and tames
The spirit's light, to seek an entrance there.
But ye whose body and soul have equal growth
And bear Love's blest baptismal mark in both,
   Whether for joy the years seem scarce enough,
Or else to resignation doomed, but loth,
Approach Love's holy guild, and learn the oath,
   Free of the secret brotherhood of Love.

XXVII.

CAN this our Love, as the old sage dared to deem,
    Be but soft prelude to some grand choral strain,
    A first link in the interminable chain
That penetrates the world's eternal scheme ?
Ah could I credit the transcendent dream,
    Then clothed in glory, hand in hand, we twain
    Should be exalted on from reign to reign
Till throned on truth above the things that seem.
But love so pure would be a solitude.
    To love the good alone, no more love thee ;
    Rather would I be bound than so made free,
And rather have, by human doubt pursued,
    A human heart to which my soul might flee
And fold her wings and dream, though dreams delude.

XXVIII.

WHAT though I tread the thorny path of pain
    With feet unhardened by the soiling years;
   What though I keep the well of endless tears
Warm in a heart time's frosts would seal in vain;
What though the toil, the hunger, and the stain
    Have half defaced my likeness to my peers,
   That scarce it seems my own face that appears
In the dim troubled mirror of my brain;
Yet, love, for thee, yet, love, for thy dear grace,
    I walk in dreams as t'ward the morning star,
      Through clouds that shine and open out above;
And all the future flames about my face,
    And all the past lies looming low afar
      To me emerging on the heights of love.

XXIX

SWEETEST, I have not slept these two nights past
    For dreaming of thy deep delicious eyes.
  I have not slept . youth, mystic, rapturous, lies
By Love and Hope ; but manhood sees the vast
Dim formless future of love overcast,
    The clear hard iron-blue of awful skies,
    Where dismal starlight with deep darkness vies,
That bodes of death and severance at the last.
So manhood lies upon his anguished couch
    'Neath Love the pale Destroyer's brooding wings,
      Mingling high ecstasies with dreams of Death.
Dim Fear and tortured Pity by him crouch,
      And wild regret her hands in anguish wrings,
      And frantic Desolation gasps for breath

XXX.

YES thou must die : I can but borrow thee.
　　Nettles are flowering on some destined grave
　By oozy sands the salt seas ever lave,
Or 'neath some black-blue crawling cedar tree
Where the grass withers.　Moaning winds at sea
　And sobbing waters, wave on heart-sick wave,
　Disconsolate, persistent, sigh and rave,
And dark leaves rustle where thy bed must be.
Yes thou must die—die ?　Spread the shroud and pall.
　The grave, the grave is the one marriage-bed :
　　The grave it is my heart is set upon
Thou art the grave : in thee are summed up all
　Its horror and regret.　To lose thee—dead ?
　　Dead, dead—why must I love thee ?—dead and gone.

XXXI

I envy not the lovers who are glad,
   Whose happy faces, foolish, fair, and fond,
  Are mirrored in the narrow village-pond
As placid as their lives ; who wax not sad
With the deep mysteries wherein life is clad,
   Who see the long years multiply love's bond,
   And dream of other life and love beyond,
And know not, being fools, that they are mad.
In sight of death we sit, and kiss and sigh,
   Mid myrtles with a cedar-shade above,
     Bound to each other by a mournful spell.
What joy were worth the solemn ecstasy,
   The bitterness of our funereal love
     Where each kiss is a lingering farewell

XXXII.

AS I go musing through this mournful land
    Soothed by the pine-tree's solemn harmony,
  Thy well-loved image comes and walks by me.
I seem to hold thee by the gentle hand
And talk of things I dimly understand,
    That thy dear spirit set to mine may be
    As to an intricate lock the simple key,
That knows it, and can move its iron band.
Then, when the torrent's music bids me wake,
    And I stand staring at the purple hills,
Alone, and at the pine-woods and the lake,
I feel as one whom tears nor dreams can slake;
    The sweet past with despair the future fills;
Hope like a half-healed wound begins to ache.

XXXIII.

AY as from dreams of some old glorious fight,
    Flags flying, and shaken steel, and mounds of slain,
  A soldier starts, and feels his old wound pain
His tossing side. anon he sits upright
And rubs his lonely eyes in the dim night,
    The glorious vision fading from his brain :
    Only the sullen-throbbing pangs remain,
The unforgetful wound, the tear-dimmed sight.
So ofttimes having wandered in my sleep
    By those loved lanes and hedgerows to our tryst,
I press the lids of thy great eyes, and weep
To feel against my heart thy wild heart leap
    Once more—Night yawns—Where are the eyes I kissed ?
The heart-aches and the tears are all I keep.

XXXIV

THY picture's lips of mute and moveless art
  Are unto me an eloquent despair.
I call them fondest names in many a prayer,
I press them to my own : they will not part.
No sudden laughters from their stillness start,
  No fluttering chase of words through the bright air
  Breaks from their fencèd covert ; yet they wear
The very language of thy love-taught heart.
Music that ere it can be hearkened dies,
  A sweetness half-suspected in the brain :—
So the faint Arab lifting his weak eyes
Sees like a cruel laughter mocking rise
  The glitter of shining water along the plain,
And phantom palms that beckon from the skies.

XXXV.

A garden ransacked of its fairest rose,
   A heaven denuded of its chiefest star
  Is life without thee : fatal flaws that mar
Miraculous jewels ; veins, the sculptor's foes
In marble , evil dreams in sweet repose
   Leave not, each in its kind, so deep a scar ;
   At no time do the heavens seem so far,
And flowers I look upon appear to close.
Ay, as one reading in a volume sage
   With thoughts that wander, starts at length to find
   No meaning enter in his vacant mind,
Only his eyes stare at the lettered page ;
So I, whom sad absorbing wants engage,
   After long looking know that I am blind.

XXXVI.

A cut rose set in water, poor sick wraith,
　　Survives a little while in hectic bloom,
　A ghostly body in a living tomb :
E'en as a love-sick maid it lingereth
Feeding its passion with protracted death ;
　　While through the very wound that wrought its doom
　It draws unnatural nourishment : the room
Is long time fragrant with its dying breath.
How slow life droops away cut off from thee,
　But cannot wither, though inch by inch it dies '
Torn cruelly from love's mutilated tree,
　Through my heart's wound I drink what grief supplies
Of waterish sustenance, salt as the sea ;
　And all the night is heavy with my sighs.

XXXVII

WHY in her absence doth the world appear
    As void of her, a vacant wilderness ?
  E'en while thou sighest the shiver of her dress
Makes blessèd music in each happier ear
About her home.   Why feed on gloom and fear
  As earth were empty of her loveliness ?
  Set rather all thy loving mind to guess ?
Her sweet seclusion, as when thou art near.
Still thy belovèd rises every morn,
  And in the holy stillness of her room
    Dresses her dainty beauty at the glass ;
And, while thy tears divide the night forlorn,
  Her soft light heart-beats in the breathing gloom
    Record the maiden moments as they pass.

XXXVIII.

LOOSED from strange hands into the wet wild night
  Straight to his home the carrier-dove returns :
  The faithful love that in his bosom burns
Is as a lamp to guide his lonely flight :
He lingers not where sheltering boughs invite,
  Nor backward from the gathering tempest turns,
  Till far off in the distance he discerns
At the known casement the familiar light.
How many miles hath my poor spirit flown
  This night to thee through wind and storm and rain,
    Bearing thee words of many mystic things,
Till thou on thy soft pillow making moan
  Didst hear it pecking at thy lattice pane,
    And took it in, a dove with draggled wings.

XXXIX.

EACH fair familiar feature of thy face
    Shines through the darkness where my soul abides
  As on the bridegroom's love-bright eye the bride's,
Or dimly through the pillared outer space,
Forth of the rich remotest holy place,
    Between the o'er-arching sculptured temple-sides,
    A taper, like a star the cloud half hides,
Lends each pale worshipper a little grace.
Ah cold the frozen marble to my knees,
    Cold, cold; but warm the heart that prays. Still show
    Thy face forth of the chancel to me here.
Still shine upon me darkling, where I freeze
      Here in thine outer courts and pray, one glow
      To lend my labouring soul a little cheer.

XL.

THE wanderer, journeying through the midnight wood,
    Belated, gladdens when the boughs that bar
  His sight of heaven, parting, disclose a star ;
And, cheered by the small beam, in happier mood
Pursues his path for many a lonely rood :
    Nay, quickened by that one, though faint and far,
    He dreams how bright a host its brethren are,
And in the dream his lonely heart finds food.
So have I made life's journey many a mile,
    Through all its tangled brakes and weary ways,
    Bearing a light within my heart for days,—
Some sweet word in a letter, some love-wile,
    Some grateful thanks, some valued scrap of praise,
Some fond remembered look, or treasured smile.

XLI.

MY heart's love is a miser, and his hoard
    Gold coins of memory, that bear for print
   My lady's effigy stamped at love's own mint
In various posture : words, too, that record
Her praises and Love's power as sovereign lord
    Of me and man by God's grace : which, by dint
    Of boundless usury and narrow stint,
Lie in my secret heart securely stored.
Ah when in silent night the door is fast
    And privacy assured, with what sweet greed
      I draw them forth from their close hiding-place
And count my treasures !—joys earned in the past
    And saved forever, precious word and deed,
      And untold fabulous riches of her grace.

XLII.

THE sweet-souled instrument in silence stands
    And yearns for the musician, far apart,
  To thaw the music frozen round its heart
With the caress of his miraculous hands.
It dreams of him astray in other lands :
    Long silence cannot kill its tones, that start
    To life again at once, touched by his art
Who alone feels with it and understands.
So bides my heart in silence (ah too long)
    For thee, and will not yield that secret tone
To others which to thee must still belong.
Yet I forget not how the notes should throng,
    Thee I forget not dreaming here alone.
Touch me, and I shall blossom into song.

XLIII.

MUSIC and love are surely next of kin ;
    For when by mystery of vague stars I hear
  Love-song and lute-lay wafted o'er the mere
Timed by the plash of oars ; or when begin
The thrilling pulses of the violin
    To vibrate in the chamber of mine ear ,
    Then can I never check the rising tear,
And my hand misses thine to nestle in.
Yes, on the storm of orchestras, the might
    Of the tempestuous plumes of choral song,
    Thy form arises winged ; an angel throng
Surrounds it, clouds beneath it : waves of light
    Throb through the living air grown swift and strong
As sea-waves maddened with the storm's delight.

XLIV.

$\mathbf{A}$S when day upon weary day it rains
        For weeks in summer, roused at early morn
    From pleasant dreams into a world forlorn
By the drops rattling on the window panes, ,
We curse the light, that brings us no new gains
    But tedious hours till wearied and outworn
    We sink again to sleep, as vainly born ;
And, weary of life itself, the soul complains.
E'en such a curse the brightest day appears
    To me at times, when the new-risen sun
    Tells me, new-wakened, of a day begun
Wherein thy voice shall never reach mine ears.
    Then I could wish for night, and labour done,
And loneliness, and the relief of tears.

XLV.

A S the faint ghost of a forgotten strain
    Haunts the deserted chambers of the mind:
  A restless presence, dreamlike, undefined ;
A spirit the hands of flesh grasp all in vain,
Elusive of the embrace that would detain
  Its phantom flight, formless and fleet as wind,
  Down thought's long echoing corridors , though behind
Some lingering sense of it may still remain.
Such is the past of lovers : dear delight,
  Sweet lips that kissed sweet eyes that wept for me—
Oh follow not their fleet and phantom flight
Through all the winding labyrinths of the night !
  The noiseless doors close on them as they flee
Out of the dream into the waking light.

XLVI.

I saw thee in a vision of the night
   Transfigured ; for it seemed that on thy brows
   The heavens did rest with all their stars, like boughs
Laden with blossoms ; round thy feet the bright
Green waves, like grass, ran rippling, strewn with white
   Star-fragments of rent petals : wasted vows,
   And ruined prayers I thought them, such as house
In hearts that love and are not loved aright.
Then all whom unrequited love had slain
   Like fallen coins gathered the shining stars,
     Scraping them from between thy callous feet,
And held them up to thee with moans of pain,
   Their bosoms famine-ribbed as with deep scars,
     Crying, " We starve : give us to drink and eat."

XLVII.

IS not this cruel that thou, poor child, must look
　　Upon my torment; thou whose piteous breast
　Would heave at sight of a bird's rifled nest ;
Thou, whom with violent sobs the tear-storm took
But at a tale of sorrow in a book ,
　　And canst not give me my soul's one request,
　　The true assurance that thou lov'st me best,
The heart another's ruthless treachery took.
We are as famished mariners on a wreck,
　　And sit and stare into each others eyes,
　　　Helpless to give the draught they dumbly crave ;
Beneath us but the dry and sapless deck,
　　Above us but the bare and burning skies,
　　　And all the while we drift towards the grave.

XLVIII.

L^O the same moon, that lights one dreamy sky,
    Doth look upon two lovers, as they stray
  By a calm stream through the yet unmown hay,
Where the still gleaming surface slipping by
Mirrors the trustful cheek, so soft and shy,
    At rest on the strong shoulder   and that ray
    Makes legible the letters that betray
The secret of a suicide's agony.
These two men loved her: in their horoscope
    One love-light shines with mocking tenderness
      On this one's brief delight, that other's tomb.
So is it ever;—Paradise laid ope
    For twain ; but outside in the wilderness
      A third soul wanders through eternal gloom.

XLIX.

HOW canst thou shape thy lips to call me friend ?
　　Doth not thy heart, turned rebel at that name,
　Plant on thy cheek the sanguine flag of shame
In red revolt, bidding thee make an end
Of the false traitor words that so offend,
　　’Gainst love’s true heirs urging a spurious claim,
　Usurpers of his titles and his fame,
Partakers of his kingdom, which they rend.
Nay rather let the cold oblivion seal
　　Each gentle act that clasps me to thy breast,
　　And let my features fade out of thy thought.
Nay, either knight me lover where I kneel,
　Or pierce me with the sword : so shall I rest—
　　To thee I must be all in all, or nought.

L.

THE darkness swallows up the feeble light,
    And the great silence gulfs the still small sound ;
  And little love in lasting time lies drowned
Five fathom deep and buried out of sight ·
But the great beacon makes a day in night,
    And echoes, that from breast to breast rebound
    Of mountains at their granite joys, astound
The shrinking valleys with their loud delight.
Hold up thy head, poor swimmer among the waves,
    Warm waves that rock thee in their wild embrace :
      The still cold depths are underneath thee now.
There the dim ooze scarce creeps between the graves,
    Where wind nor sun shall visit the pale face,
      Nor wave shall stir a tress on the dead brow.

LI.

I dreamed that twixt two fair far-sundered spheres
　　A bridge of beams was wrought with starry twire,
　That arched and wound in many a radiant spire
Across the gulf of the unpeopled years;
And o'er the bridge, like living loves and fears,
　Went wild-eyed wingèd things, and shapes of fire,
　Despairs that wrung their hands for doomed desire,
And sheeted forms that shed eternal tears.
Ah well I knew those peopled planets, well
　The folk that passed between them, full of woe
　　And lamentations, and tears poured in vain:
And Love it was who thus linked heaven with hell,
　And let the phantom thoughts go to and fro,
　　My soul and thine across this gulf of pain.

LII.

$\mathbf{A}$S fresh and faded leaves grow on one tree
    In wintry summer, ere its prime be sped;
  As gold and grey hairs on one hapless head
Where youth is mixed with sorrow; as you see
Two children lying on one mother's knee,
    One full of rosy life, one cold and dead;
  As bright and dark thoughts on each other tread
Through some fair mind made mad with misery:
So is my heart's true love both young and old,
And fresh May green, and August's tarnished gold,
    Sprinkled most strangely, in its July meet.
Ah me, to think my summer is so cold,
And soon, so soon, must I, frost-bound, behold
    All my young dreams fall shaken to my feet.

LIII

AS a flower springs up out of dark and cold,
   Drawn by the gracious beauty of the light,
  A bud that knows not all its own delight,
Till opening to one blaze of red and gold
Its deep-involvèd splendours, fold by fold,
   It yields the perfume of its being one night,
   Touches with conscious joy its nature's height,
Then withers back into the crumbling mould :
So love from the human spirit's lonely lair,
   Nourished in moving darkness and damp gloom ;
And peeps forth shyly to the golden air,—
   A mere bud, but a blossom in its womb,
   That knows itself a moment of brief bloom,
Then withers back into the soul's despair

LIV.

WAVE after wave arises from the deep,
　　And slips back into silence and the grave :
　　It matters not whether it fret and rave
And foam at lip with fury, or still keep
A quiet motion · both sink into sleep,
　　The same cold sleep, and the great sea, that gave,
　　Receives again their life, wave after wave.
Shall we who think of it give thanks or weep ?
I know not ; only would the law not lay
　　With love as life ! for as our lives emerge
　　From the vague sea to sing their own brief dirge ;
So out of each of these, and vain as they,
　　Love after love arises like a surge,
And sighs, and passes in the sigh away.

LV.

OH river flowing through the silent night
    Murmuring beneath the moon, while we in sleep
  Lie careless, thou, unresting, still dost keep
Thy constant course.   And in our souls a flight
With more of mystery in its noiseless might
    Keeps pace with thine towards a deeper deep.
    Dream on, ye dreamers : could ye wake and weep
Ye would not stay nor keep that stream in sight.
Its waves slip from us silently one by one,
    Whether we stand and watch them, or forget
In dreamless sleep ; still through our soul they run.
    Each sighs in passing, "Welcome,—hail,—well met,—
    Farewell,—adieu ;" a gladness, a regret ;
A future, and a past ; beginning, done.

LVI.

AS wine is sweet of taste to eager lips;
  And as to him who hath well drunk it seems
 A deep sea traversed by the wings of dreams
And thoughts, like full-blown sails of mighty ships,
That come out from between the hornèd tips
  Of a great moon asleep on solemn streams,
  That low by the glass-rimmed horizon beams;—
But afterwards is darkness and eclipse :
So seems the magic wine, that love outpours,
  To souls that quaff the madness of its grapes,
A sea, where dream-birds visit the dim shores,
And barques with swell of sails and sweep of oars
  Come out of the great light, that grows, and shapes
Its crescent to a sphere by death's dark doors.

LVII.

LIKE as a stream, that, having climbed a hill
    A little lower than its watershed,
   Thinking adown a steeply-sloping bed
Upon the further side to race and rill
Fed with new speed, stays suddenly and still,
    Discouraged and amazed, finding instead
   A level plateau ; and with force unfed
Flows languid on, too weak to turn a mill :
So oft my spirit shaping thee to sight
    Hath hoped to climb the red-lit clouds of song
     With plumes flame-tipped from fire-sprayed surge of
                 (dreams,
But droops, her force spent in that first sea-flight,
    And flaps with weak and labouring wings along
    The level flats of weary souls and streams.

LVIII.

OH let me dream !   Let slumber draw the bars
    That keep me in my prison.   Oh to gloat,
  Changed to a bird, upon my own sweet note !
Where no least wind the placid level mars
To lie and dabble 'mong the nenuphars,
    Changed to a swan, by mere or castle-moat !
    In purple air on filmy wings to float
Between the silent sea and solemn stars !
To swim with the moon over and under me
    Upon the bosom of a tide unknown !
        To thrid a fairy city by star-beams !
In a dim cave below the musical sea
    To meet my lady loving and alone !
        To feel her voice within my spirit !—Dreams.

LIX.

OH to live like a pictured pastoral !
  To lie on grass-crowned crags stretched out at ease
  O'er the ripple-shrunk wave- meshes of the seas,
In the fresh dawn, trolling a madrigal,
And hear the kids bleat to their dams' far call !
  To drowse at noon under spread abute trees
  And watch the village girls with their brown knees
Bring pitchers to the well, limber and tall !
By shade of wrecked Corinthian art soft-kissed,
  When the fierce light makes the far hills unseen,
And the river fades into a silver mist,
    By one more gentle than her lambs to loll,
    By the water-side, upon a wooded knoll !
To dance to pipe and tabour on the green.

LX.

TO list vague music float o'er moonlit meres,
    The drowsy county-cries at dim day-break ;
  To gaze on purple distance till it make
Our spirit pine to dwell beyond the spheres ;
To pause in starlight by dim river-weirs,
    To think of the beloved half-awake
   Till all the yearning breast bitterly ache,
And the o'erburdened heart find ease in tears ;
Is it not pain ? To drink immortal songs ;
    To pulse with ecstasy at heroic deeds ;
     To look on glories we may ne'er attain ;
What quality in common here belongs
    Which draws from us that blood the spirit bleeds
     In all supreme delight ? Is it not pain ?

LXI.

IN sleep I saw the skies at midnight red
   From the zenith to the ocean's fevered lips,
  And all the dark tide blush with blazing ships
And burning towns.   Fierce flames, suddenly shed,
Each like a snake lifting its crested head,
   Sprang from the isles far-scattered : dull eclipse
   Shadowed the stars : the blurred moon's hornèd tips,
Weltering through wreathèd fog-smoke, oozed and bled.
Heaven, sea, and earth in wild confusion burned,
   And by that light I saw pale mothers fling
    Their babes on the sharp rocks from cliffs above.
Then to a cloaked shape at my side I turned,
   And questioned it, "What fiend hath done this thing ?"
   And it replied "These are the deeds of Love."

LXII.

OH heart, why wilt thou suffer evermore ?
    What is thy limit of endurance ?   Spray
  Rends rocks, and rust eats iron bars away ;
But thou, though yearlong thus afflicted sore,
Art not consumed : but as the rough-ribbed shore,
    Tide-washed and worn, of some wave-eaten bay,
    Repairs the sea's destruction day by day,
Thou art renewed, abiding as before
Is it that some diviner element
    Hath made thee proof against earth's frets and jars
      That thou dost so o'er-tax this body and brain ?
      Or is it that, seeing some light beyond the strain,
    Thou with thy gaze fixed somewhere on the stars
Abidest still in a severe content ?

LXIII

THE office of the strong is to console,
    And the heart's purest joy ; freely to take
  A world's woes on thee ; with kind words to slake
The sick heart of a brother, to make whole
The mind's disease, despair, and to condole
    By brave example with the weak :—forsake
    Thyself for this, thou from ill dreams shalt wake,
A great peace growing up within thy soul.
Tears for another's pain are salve for thine,
    And water not the spirits dastard weeds
    As tears shed for thyself, but nurse the seeds
Of high resolve : this sovereign anodyne
    In souls sincere begets those words and deeds
So human that man names them best divine.

LXIV.

WHEN in the lonely stillness of the tomb
   I voiceless lie and cold, omit not thou
To sing and dance as merrily as now :
Bring roses once a year in fullest bloom,
And rather than that thou shouldst come in gloom,
   Bring thy new love with thee : together bow
   O'er the green mound that hides the quiet brow—
Yea I would bless his babe within thy womb.
How can love be where jealousy is not ?
   How shall I say ?   This only: I have borne
That cruel pain : yet would I never blot,
Living, with selfish love the loved-one's lot,
   Nor, dead, would have my dear love live forlorn,—
Yet would not wish my own love quite forgot.

www.ingramcontent.com/pod-product-compliance
Lightning Source LLC
Chambersburg PA
CBHW061048050726
47592CB00004B/1622